BUYER BEWARE

BASTARDRY IN THE BODY CORPORATE

MICHAEL ANDREW

BUYER BEWARE: BASTARDRY IN THE BODY CORPORATE
First published in Australia in 2022 by Michael Andrew

© Michael Andrew 2022

A catalogue record for this book is available from the National Library of Australia

ISBN 978-0-6454303-0-1 (pbk)

Editing by Helena Bond
Cover design & typesetting by Sharon Felschow, dta studio
Printed by Ingram Spark

What we ignore, we empower.

— *Chris CUOMO, CNN anchor*

Acknowledgements

I would like to take this opportunity to acknowledge the professional work achieved by my editor, Helena Bond. Her assistance in producing this book has been second to none.

I would also like to thank my book designer, Sharon Felschow, who has turned this book into a piece of art.

Thank you to the both of you.

Contents

INTRODUCTION

In my early 50s I downsized into a two-bedroom apartment on the coast of South-East Queensland. The move took me out of my dream house, where I'd been living happily with my daughter, into one of 74 apartments. I was looking for a lower maintenance lifestyle — I'd been invalided from the NSW Police Service with a knee injury — and for some peace and quiet as I aged.

Sadly, like many people moving from freehold to strata dwelling, what I found was a much higher stress life, due to the actions and lack of action of the body corporate — both the committee and the complex managers.

But first, a bit of background. Born in 1962, I am the fifth child and fourth son of an aircraft fitter in the Royal Australian Air Force. I was born in the British Military Hospital in Tai Ping, Malaya (now Malaysia), and after relocating several times between Malaya and Australia, my family settled in the western suburbs of Sydney, where my father began civilian life as a real estate agent.

I was an average student, but I was good enough to enter the New South Wales Police Force on 25 February 1980. I became a probationary constable in 1981, and was confirmed as a Constable of Police in 1982. During my service, I was stationed at seven different stations, as well as the Transport Branch. My knee was injured on the job, which ultimately resulted in my medical discharge from the NSW Police Service.

In the early 2000s, I was granted full custody of my then four-year-old daughter. We moved to Queensland, where we built our dream house, and then — well, that's where this all began.

My time in the New South Wales Police Force conditioned me not only to abide by laws, but also to abide by community expectations, and behave in a moral and ethical manner. Little did I know the amount of corruption, bullying and attempted intimidation I would encounter in my apartment block's body corporate committee. And the fact that they documented the extent of their corruption in the committee minutes — with the assistance of the body corporate managers — defies belief. This book details my experience of the committee; I hope it will let people make a better educated decision on how, or whether, to engage with similar bodies corporate.

Everybody who owns an apartment at the complex that I am rechristening 'The Apartments' is a lot owner and is therefore a member of the body corporate. There is also a committee comprised of seven people. The committee runs the place, directing both the body corporate managers and the complex managers.

In addition, there are body corporate managers who organise committee and general meetings, including the agendas and minutes of the meetings. They attend all meetings. I refer to them throughout as ECS (Expensive Corporate Secretaries) since I would be risking a libel lawsuit if I named them. Although I believe I have sufficient evidence to win such a suit, I don't intend to waste any more of my time on them.

You should note though that as of July 2021, the legislation for defamation changed. A company that employs 10 or more people is now limited in what legal proceedings they can commence against persons for defamation. Therefore, although I could actually name them without fear of prosecution, and also the lawyers from whom they seek their advice, I will follow my own lawyer's advice, and I will not name them.

This book focuses mainly on the committee and their actions, though the body corporate managers were also involved in most of the incidents. Again, identifying details have been changed to protect the guilty and avoid a lawsuit. As membership of the committee changes over the years, and since the committee members who participated in each situation clearly believed they were above the law — omnipotent, even — I have drawn their pseudonyms from the better-known Greek, Roman and Norse deities. I've also replaced calendar years with years relating to my tenure at The Apartments, so Year 1 is the year I moved in, and Year 8 is the year I moved out, vowing never to return.

There are also complex managers, as approximately 50% of the apartments are holiday lets, that is, short-term accommodation. A couple of the apartments are long-term rentals, and the remainder are owner–occupiers. The complex manager's duties are outlined in an agreement with the body corporate committee.

Before you read on, I must stipulate that this book deals with owning and residing at the apartment complex; not with the holiday rental business conducted at the complex. This book in no way reflects on that business. It illustrates the old saying: lovely place to visit; wouldn't want to live there.

Also, let me say that all the personnel I dealt with at the Office of the Commissioner of Body Corporate and Community Management were terrific. From the conciliators to the staff answering the phone calls in relation to aspects of the law, they were all professional, friendly and cannot be faulted. I do indeed thank them, and appreciate their service.

1

THE COMMITTEE AND ITS WORK

What is a body corporate committee?

Theory

In Australia, when different owners live in separate lots on freehold land that also has some common property, they are required to manage it through a body corporate and a management statement. This arrangement is commonly referred to as "strata title" being managed by a "body corporate". The laws, and the terminology used, vary from state to state. In Queensland law, "strata title" is officially a "community title scheme", but no-one ever calls it that, and nor shall I.

A body corporate exists — under the *Body Corporate and Community Management Act 1997 (Qld)*, hereafter referred to as the BCCM Act — to "provide for flexible and contemporary communally based arrangements for the use of freehold land". It is supposed to administer the common property and body corporate assets for the benefit of lot owners and enforce the community management statement (including any by-laws). It should also act reasonably, balance the rights of individuals with the responsibility for self-management of the scheme; encourage the tourism potential of schemes without diminishing the rights and responsibilities of lot owners; provide an appropriate level of consumer protection for owners and intending buyers of lots; ensure access to information about issues; and provide an efficient and effective dispute resolution process. The role of the body corporate is usually carried out by a committee, made up of lot owners.

The committee is subject to a code of conduct, which is stipulated in the BCCM Act, and reproduced here. All committee members should perform their duties while upholding these six clauses.

Schedule 1A: Code of conduct for committee voting members

1) Commitment to acquiring understanding of Act, including this code

   A committee voting member must have a commitment to acquiring an understanding of this Act, including this code of conduct, relevant to the member's role on the committee.

2) Honesty, fairness and confidentiality

   (1) A committee voting member must act honestly and fairly in performing the member's duties as a committee voting member.

   (2) A committee voting member must not unfairly or unreasonably disclose information held by the body corporate, including information about an owner of a lot, unless authorised or required by law to do so.

3) Acting in body corporate's best interests

   A committee voting member must act in the best interests of the body corporate in performing the member's duties as a committee voting member, unless it is unlawful to do so.

4) Complying with Act and this code

   A committee voting member must take reasonable steps to ensure the member complies with this Act, including this code, in performing the member's duties as a committee voting member.

> 5) Nuisance
>
>   A committee voting member must not—
>
>   (a) cause a nuisance on scheme land; or
>
>   (b) otherwise behave in a way that unreasonably affects a person's lawful use or enjoyment of a lot or common property.
>
> 6) Conflict of interest
>
>   A committee voting member must disclose to the committee any conflict of interest the member may have in a matter before the committee.

Practice

What I found was an almost complete disregard for the code of conduct, or the BCCM Act itself. Let me walk you through my experience …

Repairs

Theory

The committee should take care of the day-to-day maintenance and repairs needed in the common areas of the complex. The committee looks after the budget, and directs the complex managers, who live on site, to arrange repairs or servicing of items such as the pool, pool filter, elevators, etc. They also recommend which building managers to engage, which electrical contractor to contract for supply of electricity to the building, etc. The committee usually meets four times a year; however, if something of a more serious nature arises, they organise a "voting outside committee meeting". This incurs extra costs, so is not something to be done on a whim.

Within a body corporate, the committee holds a surprising amount of power. They can levy hundreds of thousands of dollars from ordinary members and make decisions that affect people's health, safety, and the value of their homes.

Practice

It was hard to get anything repaired through the committee. On two occasions I submitted correspondence and/or motions to be tabled about repairs, only to find they had "gone missing". Whether the body corporate managers didn't do their job and add the correspondence to the agenda or whether they were under instruction from the committee not to include it, I simply do not know. In either case, it would be a breach of the BCCM Act and clause 4 of its code of conduct.

Even when members' correspondence did get brought to the committee's attention, there was often no result. It didn't seem to matter how important the issue was, or how many people were affected.

For example, the fire alarm system needed both repairs and maintenance. This, of course, is a safety issue. The fire alarm speakers in my apartment — along with those in quite a few others — did not work. At the same time, three units needed windows replaced, due to minor leaks when it rained. This was a convenience issue, not a safety issue. Two of the units belonged to committee members. Guess what got repaired first? It wasn't the fire alarm system!

I call that a clear breach of the BCCM Act, code of conduct, clause 3. Surely repairs to the building-wide fire safety system should be the first priority of the committee!

Furthermore, two maintenance issues that affected my property were not dealt with during the entire time I lived at the complex.

When I moved in, I discovered that my exclusive use car space was often flooded. Naturally, I applied to have this fixed. The car stood in water, and I also had to stand in the water to access the car or boot. After a conciliation process, $20,000 was set aside in the budget for water ingress remediation. But in the 7 years I resided at the complex, nothing was done.

Much later, I also applied to have water damage to my kitchen repaired — the balcony above mine leaked in Year 6. The cost of fixing my kitchen was only $220. The quote, which I obtained from a company who at the time were painting the outside of the building, also identified that the leak was coming from above my apartment. However, nothing had been repaired by the time I left the complex in Year 8.

You know what? Paris's Eiffel Tower took only 2 years, 2 months, and 5 days to complete.

To me, failing to make these repairs over such a long time constitutes a breach of the BCCM Act, code of conduct, clause 2(1). It was neither honest nor fair to delay the repairs, despite all my attempts to get them fixed, or at least mitigated.

Application of by-laws

Theory

Each body corporate makes a set of rules that residents of the complex must abide by. These are known as the by-laws. Typical by-laws cover what happens if body corporate members fail to pay their levies, what pets may be allowed and under what conditions, where washing may be hung, and other such vital matters.

You would think that a major responsibility of the body corporate committee would be ensuring that these by-laws are upheld consistently throughout the complex. But no.

Practice

In my experience at The Apartments, it soon became obvious that committee members did not think that the BCCM Act, or the by-laws for the apartment complex, applied to them. It was "one rule for us (committee members) and another rule for them (other lot owners)".

The Merriam-Webster online dictionary defines "corruption" as "dishonest or illegal behaviour especially by powerful people (such as government officials or police officers)". The Cambridge online dictionary defines "corruption" as "illegal, bad or dishonest behaviour, especially by people in positions of power".

Let's look at some examples. On one occasion, the Secretary of the committee, at that time Venus, wanted to upgrade her air conditioning system by adding an additional air conditioning unit. The BCCM Act stipulates that when an improvement of a lot on exclusive use common property (such as the air conditioner's compressor) exceeds $3,000, body corporate permission should be sought at a general meeting. Instead, she had it installed and then had the matter ratified at the next committee meeting. At no stage was it put before the body corporate general membership for their approval; it was "approved" at committee level, which is illegal.

So that breaches clause 4 of the code of conduct, which requires committee members to comply with the Act and code.

On another occasion, a committee member wanted to install an enclosed cage next to his exclusive use car space. This also required body corporate approval, and in this case the owner submitted the required paperwork. It was voted on at the annual general meeting, and turned down. Despite this, the committee member went ahead and installed the cage anyway, thereby thumbing their nose at every member of the body corporate! When the committee turned a blind eye to this behaviour, they effectively sanctioned this scandalous lack of regard for The Apartments' by-laws, a further breach of clause 4.

This same committee member was also responsible for a complaint by the solicitors at the front of the building. The committee member constantly parked his campervan on level G, which was the domain of the solicitors. The solicitors were paying for exclusive use car spaces, yet the committee member continued to park his van there. Several emails were sent from the solicitors to the body corporate managers, ECS, yet nothing was done. I was shocked to find that the minutes of the February Year 7 meeting noted that no examples of breaches had been notified by the solicitors. But this was a case of falsifying the records of the meeting, as the solicitors had made plenty of specific complaints, as well as providing photographic evidence.

Please note that whilst the committee member referred to was not a committee member at the time of the parking complaints by the solicitors at the front of the building, he was a committee member both prior to and after the complaints. So he knew what to do. Or should have known.

When I submitted a motion for the Secretary to be issued with a breach notice (for breaching the code of conduct), I also attached various photos of illegal parking of vehicles belonging to either committee members or their spouses; no action had ever been taken against the owners of those particular vehicles. Yet when the committee did get around to disciplining someone for parking, as recorded in the February Year 7 minutes, they chose to take action against a member of the body corporate who was **not** a member of the committee.

The committee did whatever they wanted, wherever they wanted, yet no other person was allowed to do the same: pure hypocrisy.

Dealing with nuisances

Theory

The body corporate committee is supposed to uphold the by-laws to make life in a shared complex pleasant for everyone.

Practice

In practice, committee members did as they pleased, regardless of the effect of their actions on other residents.

In a further breach of the BCCM Act, code of conduct, clause 5(a), committee member's spouses were responsible for a number of unpleasant incidents. In one, there was apparently an apartment that was generating some noise. The then Secretary's husband, Mars, attended reception and made a complaint … for over four-and-a-half minutes. As far as I'm aware, it only takes about 10–30 seconds to make a noise complaint. This was a full-blown rant! I have video — with audio — of this incident.

On another occasion, I shared an elevator with Mars and another conflict occurred, which I recorded on my laptop.

There was also a committee member's husband who liked to abuse guests. So much so that at least one guest registered her complaint on Google Maps about the incident.

Running for office

Theory

Running for membership on a body corporate committee is very similar to running for office to become a member of parliament. You outline what the opposition has done, their faults and performance, then make your campaign promises about what you are willing to do to help the body corporate. It's just like Labor v the Liberal National Party in Australia, Democrats v Republicans in the USA, or Labour v Conservatives in the UK.

Practice

In principle, if the body corporate committee is not serving its purpose well, other members are able to step in to replace the committee and get back on track. But doing so is truly a hard slog.

When a group of lot owners got together to challenge the sitting committee, the then Secretary, Artemis, sent around an email, of which there are extracts below. I was running for Chairperson, and as you can see, she had a good go at me.

Actually, to be fair, the mud-slinging you're about to read really does resemble many political campaigns!

From: Artemis

Subject: Poor Candidate Behaviour

Good Afternoon

It is with sincere dismay that I find myself writing this letter … if these candidates need to treat you like a 2-year-old and fill out your ballot paper for you and also provide a pre-paid envelope addressed to [ECS], then what level have they slumped to now and what level of intelligence do they believe you have?

The past couple of months have, in my opinion, resembled that of a dirty and underhanded federal political party campaign …

The current SMILEY FACED candidates seem to be making a very conscientious effort to restrict our enjoyment of this building, create a very negative environment and create issues where there are none.

The previous committee … were removed due to overspending, poor performance and lack of information provided to members and there weren't any extenuating circumstances …

Also, why would we vote for a new Chairperson, without any experience, who is currently wasting body corporate funds to remove us from our jobs and family commitments for a day in order to retrieve a meagre $70. Why couldn't he have disputed this when it occurred, asked for a receipt or even refused to pay it and discussed it with the managers at the time. This is also the man who has blatantly kept his dog off lead many times in common areas, has intimidated the cleaning staff and reduced them to tears. Really! …

The smear campaign to attempt to remove our current complex managers seems somewhat familiar to that of the campaign used to remove our previous complex managers. When will this rubbish end? …

With this letter I have also included another contact update … I am reluctant to fill your mailboxes with junk mail as we have been received [sic.] in the past. It has come to my attention that there is a rather large rat who has taken a liking to removing the body corporate contact information sheet which has been posted on the community wall on level M. Despite our efforts over the past few months to ensure our contact details are made readily available, the rat seems to be going to great lengths to remove this information sheet every time it is replaced. This has happened on multiple occasions.

> I can be contacted on the details below if necessary, just leave a message if I am not available at the time. I have only spoken with honesty and integrity and believe that we should be giving our vote to those who will do the same.
>
> Kind Regards and apologies for the intrusion.
>
> Artemis
> Secretary

Although I admit I did walk my dog off the lead (a Pomeranian-Chihuahua cross, hardly vicious), everything else in there is false. Because I was holding the committee responsible for what they were doing, I had a target on my back and was being blamed for everything. The rumours about me still exist as well as the blame game.

Artemis obviously regretted the email, as shortly afterwards she resigned from the committee and actually moved out and away from the area.

Privacy

Theory

The Apartments' committee comprises seven persons, three of whom hold executive positions: the Chairperson, Secretary and Treasurer. When a member of the committee resigns and a vacancy is available on the committee, a notice is displayed around the building, in elevators, notice boards and the like, by the building manager. The body corporate manager (ECS) also mails out to all apartment owners a notice of vacancy, seeking any interest in filling it. If any nominees come forward, the vacancy is usually filled, and then ratified at the next committee meeting.

The personal details of the person who resigned should NEVER be displayed.

Practice

Eventually I did make it onto the committee as the Chairperson, however, I resigned almost immediately. I had attempted a full coup: controlling all executive positions on the committee, so I could actually assist people — and with a lot less hassle. I was successful only in obtaining the position of Chairperson. However, I knew I would have been only one voice in seven, which would not have enabled me to achieve what I wanted to. I would have been out-voted at every turn.

In addition, I refused to work with such dishonest people. I didn't want to be tarred with the same brush — to become guilty by association.

When I resigned, my name was included in all the public notices calling for new nominations. Why? I do not know. It was a blatant and unwarranted breach of the BCCM Act, code of conduct, clause 2(2). As The Apartments were nearly 50% short holiday lets, this was a very significant breach of my privacy.

And it wasn't just the body corporate committee involved: the complex managers at the time must have assisted in placing that notice, as only they possessed the keys to enable access to the notice boards.

Formal channels of communication

Theory

Because a body corporate committee is — theoretically at least — answerable to the whole body corporate membership, as well as obligated to comply with administrative requirements of the BCCM Act, they are required to follow quite formal processes for communication. Requests must be put to the committee in writing, meetings are formally minuted, etc.

As things had become more and more difficult between the committee and me, in June of Year 7, I wrote to ECS, requesting that committee members converse with me only at an official forum.

Practice

On 2 July Year 7, I was washing my car directly outside the bin room on the ground level, as there was a trailer parked in the designated car wash bay. The committee Chairperson, then Zeus, drove up and parked his vehicle approximately 10 metres from where I was washing my car, approached me and said (and I quote), "I'm just checking you out". This was not long after I had submitted a motion to the committee. Although this approach was in direct contravention of my request to only converse with me at an official forum, we then had a discussion. What else could I do? I wasn't about to run away, and it would have been very strange to ignore him.

As the conversation was about body corporate matters, I made contemporaneous notes of the exchange. Notes like this, made at the time or shortly after an event or action occurs, are admissible in a court of law.

I proffer a huge "thank you" to reception staff, who provided me with the security footage from G level to substantiate this incident. As the committee had previously used security footage to allege inappropriate behaviour on my part, I knew what I had to do.

On another occasion, Adonis (another committee member, now deceased), approached me as I was walking along one side of The Apartments complex. Again, despite my request to keep all discussions in official forums, we had a conversation about body corporate matters. This is another example of committee members approaching me inappropriately, although at least he did not attempt to intimidate me.

Demonstrably, committee members disregarded my request and simply continued to do as they pleased. This was evident in most of their other actions as well.

Excellent service?

Finally, in Year 7, I took the major step of serving a breach notice against the body corporate Secretary. This was a huge hassle to go through. Why did I bother? First and foremost, because I believed that while the Secretary was in place, I was not going to get my stuff fixed. I had also heard other people complain that their stuff wasn't getting fixed either. But if it was her stuff, it was not only fixed, it was fixed then ratified at the next meeting.

After a conciliation process in Year 6, when the committee agreed to fix my water ingress problem, to the annual general meeting in Year 7 when I submitted the breach motion, my water ingress problem was still no closer to being fixed, so the committee wasn't even complying with their own agreements.

I was also angry. I had been accused of impropriety over an incident where I took five sheets of toilet paper from the common toilets to clean up a mess in front of my car (which you can read all about in Chapter 3, Case study #4) … It was ridiculous, but the rumour I'd done something really stupid and inappropriate had gone right around the building: I heard one person say that they thought I had taken boxes and boxes of toilet paper! It was my chance to set the record straight.

And I'd been verbally abused by the Secretary's husband a couple of times. Both times were in the elevator where there were no witnesses, but I had made contemporaneous notes.

I'd tried to deal with each thing as it came up. Eventually, when I called the BCCM help line, the lady on the other end said serving a breach notice was the only step left. So I felt it had to be done. I wanted to remove the Secretary from the committee because she seemed to be the one really running the committee, and she had demonstrated that she was dishonest and corrupt. It was the combination of so many breaches of the code of conduct …

So, near the beginning of Year 7, I submitted a motion for the Secretary to be issued a formal notice for breaching the code of conduct on multiple grounds. This motion was for the Year 7 annual general meeting, to be voted on by the whole of the body corporate (all apartment owners). Depending on how the vote went, Venus would either be removed from her position on the committee, or remain as Secretary. But the Chairperson ruled the motion out of order, and therefore no vote took place.

My motion was raised at a "vote outside committee meeting" on 13 May Year 7. Committee members Zeus, Chairperson; Freya, Treasurer; Thetis; and Hera recorded in the minutes that:

> The Committee refute the claims made concerning any breaches made by the Secretary of [The Apartments], Venus, in carrying out the work of the Body Corporate. The Committee noted Venus has worked tirelessly over the

> years in this position and has produced excellent service outcomes during her appointment to the committee.

This statement was entered into the records and voted on (4:0 in favour) by the listed committee members.

Yet I have proved that the Secretary, Venus, had breached the BCCM Act constantly and deliberately. So if the above-mentioned committee members refute my claims they must have agreed with the decisions and actions of the Secretary. What does that say about those committee members? Surely that is a further breach of the code of conduct, this time of clause 1. Ignorance of the law has never been considered an excuse.

Last word

I should also mention the comments of another Chairperson who resigned from the committee. Thor, upon his resignation, wrote:

> You know what since the 2nd of January this year I have gone back to work because I was asked by the commissioner of police to do so. Apparently I have some expertise in dealing with high level organised crime... Well, since that time I have regularly been punched at, had guns and knives pointed at me and at the end of each day sadly I open my emails and have to deal with body corporate stuff. You know what [I have] had enough of this petty rubbish.
>
> I hereby tender my resignation from the committee and please NEVER ask me to join the kindergarten again.

2

THE BODY CORPORATE MANAGER AND COMPLEX MANAGER

What is a body corporate manager?

Theory

Body corporate managers organise the committee meetings and general meetings, including distribution of the agendas, meeting minutes, etc. They also send out levy notices, take the payments and do the bookkeeping.

A key part of their role is that they are meant to provide expert advice on the *Body Corporate and Community Management Act 1997* (the BCCM Act) so the committee as well as themselves comply with the Queensland Government legislation.

As part of the BCCM Act, there is a code of conduct for both body corporate and complex managers, much the same as there is for committee members.

Schedule 2: Code of conduct for body corporate managers and caretaking service contractors

1) Knowledge of Act, including code

    A body corporate manager or caretaking service contractor must have a good working knowledge and understanding of this Act, including this code of conduct, relevant to the person's functions.

2) Honesty, fairness and professionalism

    1) A body corporate manager or caretaking service contractor must act honestly, fairly and professionally in performing the person's functions under the person's engagement.

    2) A body corporate manager must not attempt to unfairly influence the outcome of an election for the body corporate committee.

3) Skill, care and diligence

    A body corporate manager or caretaking service contractor must exercise reasonable skill, care and diligence in performing the person's functions under the person's engagement.

4) Acting in body corporate's best interests

    A body corporate manager or caretaking service contractor must act in the best interests of the body corporate unless it is unlawful to do so.

5) Keeping body corporate informed of developments

   A body corporate manager or caretaking service contractor must keep the body corporate informed of any significant development or issue about an activity performed for the body corporate.

6) Ensuring employees comply with Act and code

   A body corporate manager or caretaking service contractor must take reasonable steps to ensure an employee of the person complies with this Act, including this code, in performing the person's functions under the person's engagement.

7) Fraudulent or misleading conduct

   A body corporate manager or caretaking service contractor must not engage in fraudulent or misleading conduct in performing the person's functions under the person's engagement.

8) Unconscionable conduct

   A body corporate manager or caretaking service contractor must not engage in unconscionable conduct in performing the person's functions under the person's engagement.

   Examples of unconscionable conduct—

   1) taking unfair advantage of the person's superior knowledge relative to the body corporate

   2) requiring the body corporate to comply with conditions that are unlawful or not reasonably necessary

3) exerting undue influence on, or using unfair tactics against, the body corporate or the owner of a lot in the scheme

9) Conflict of duty or interest

A body corporate manager or caretaking service contractor for a community titles scheme (the **first scheme**) must not accept an engagement for another community titles scheme if doing so will place the person's duty or interests for the first scheme in conflict with the person's duty or interests for the other scheme.

10) Goods and services to be supplied at competitive prices

A body corporate manager or caretaking service contractor must take reasonable steps to ensure goods and services the person obtains for or supplies to the body corporate are obtained or supplied at competitive prices.

11) Body corporate manager to demonstrate keeping of particular records

If a body corporate or its committee requested, in writing, the body corporate manager to show that the manager has kept the body corporate records as required under this Act, the manager must comply with the request within the reasonable period stated in the request.

Practice

During my time at The Apartments, the body corporate — on the recommendation of the committee — engaged a specialist body corporate manager with offices in several locations on Australia's east coast. They used the services of the Brisbane office, and as far as I know, they still do. As far as I was able to observe, the company served merely as expensive secretaries to the body corporate committee, and this is why I refer to them as ECS (Expensive Corporate Secretaries) throughout this book.

BCCM Act experts

Theory

The body corporate manager guides the body corporate committee to understand and work within the framework of the BCCM Act.

Practice

It states on ECS's website that they are experts in the legislation that covers bodies corporate: the BCCM Act. But looking at the meeting minutes, I would have to say that they do not demonstrate much expertise. There were regular and frequent breaches of legislation by the committee as outlined in this book. What's more, ECS didn't even know that a motion could be changed as long as its meaning was not altered (s105, Accommodation Module, BCCM Act, 'Amendment of motions at general meetings'): pretty simple stuff, yet they had no clue.

I don't know whether ECS gave advice at the committee meetings mentioned in this book at the time; if they did, and the committee declined to take that advice, it was not recorded anywhere that I have been able to access.

How is that not a breach of clauses 1 and 3 of the code of conduct?

In the body corporate's best interest

Theory

According to clause 4 of the code of conduct, the body corporate manager "must act in the best interests of the body corporate unless it is unlawful to do so".

Practice

Even though ECS is engaged by the body corporate, it is clear that they actually work for the body corporate committee. When conflicts occurred between the committee and a member of the body corporate, ECS assisted the committee, **not** the member of the body corporate who had the complaint. So when a member of the body corporate lodges a request for conciliation, that member must also contend with body corporate managers like ECS.

Before my conciliation in Year 6, ECS offered to assist the committee in preparing for the conciliation. They never offered me any help; I had to fend for myself. I have in my possession an email from ECS to the committee offering to help them. I emailed its writer, asking why ECS was offering assistance to the committee in preparing for the conciliation but not to me. Funnily enough, I never received any reply.

On another occasion, ECS actually assisted the committee in a most despicable and troubling situation — bordering on criminal — when I was asked to explain why I had taken "an unknown amount of toilet paper from the common toilets". Since I was a fully financial member of the body corporate and my fees partly pay for that toilet paper, I am allowed to use it. What if I used the toilet for what it was designed for? Am I to explain that I used the paper for what it was designed for too? I'll share that story in full in Chapter 4, Case study #4.

You will see that the body corporate manager would bend over backwards to assist members of the committee. In ECS's case, they even breached the BCCM Act themselves in order to assist a member of the committee. Hell, they would probably spoon feed you, hold you over their shoulder and burp you as long as you were on the committee. Everything the committee did was done with the assistance of these alleged experts in body corporate and community management, ECS.

How does ECS's choice to work for committee members against other lot owners not breach clauses 2(1) and 4 of their code of conduct?

Record-keepers

ECS appeared all too willing to help the committee obfuscate its actions and deliberations.

On 21 June Year 7 I wrote to ECS and informed them that I would only converse with members of the committee in an official forum.

Also on 21 June Year 7, I received correspondence from ECS asking me to provide information to justify my allegation about the falsification of records. The author of the request was not identified, but it is most likely to have been a committee member acting alone, as there had not been any recent committee meetings.

When I attempted to discover its author, however, ECS made no response to my request. It seemed particularly odd given that the information I was asked to provide **was already in the motion I had submitted** for the Secretary to be issued a notice for breaching the code of conduct. And committee members knew this, as they already had the motion in their possession. Why ask me for something they already had?

Long before that incident, in August Year 2, the committee had submitted a motion that committee meetings not be recorded in any way, shape or form: no audio or video equipment was to be allowed at any committee meeting. This motion was voted on at the meeting and — surprise, surprise — the motion was passed by all the committee members present: Hercules (Chairperson, and as proxy for Athena), Orpheus, Triton, Clotho, and Venus. The minutes leave the seventh committee member's whereabouts unaccounted for.

In another disturbing incident, a committee member had a private conversation with me, to let me know that something "quite bad" had been said about me within the committee. The person who informed me of this did not state what that something was, only that it was horrible. In an effort to find out what had been said about me, I applied to ECS under section 205 of the BCCM Act, and paid the prescribed fee to receive the information. But this attempt failed. The committee stated, upon advice received from their lawyers, that it was "privileged" under the BCCM Act. There are only two reasons why something can be defined as privileged under the Act: the first is if it is a communication between a lawyer and their client, and the second is if the communication is defamatory.

I then engaged the services of Vulcan Legal (not their real name) in an effort to obtain the information. This attempt also cost me money, and it also failed. Next I made a complaint to the Office of the Australian Information Commissioner under the *Privacy Act 1988* (Cth) to obtain the information. This also proved to be ineffective.

Finally, I made yet another complaint to the BCCM, paid the relevant fee and asked for it to go straight to adjudication, rather than to the standard conciliation process initially. I also asked for the complaint to be expedited. Both these requests were approved.

Unfortunately, I sold my apartment sooner than expected, and the BCCM was unable to complete my application.

Did you notice that I had to pay two fees there? One when I applied to ECS for information under Section 205, and again when I complained to BCCM. I could have spent heaps of money trying to get information! For example, I could've challenged the fact that the Chairperson ruled my motion about the Secretary breaching the code of conduct out of order at the Year 7 annual general meeting. But where do you stop?

At no stage was I given the information that I requested, which was simply a copy of all emails that included any mention of myself from 22 February Year 7.

In July Year 7, the committee passed another motion: that privileged information shall remain as privileged information to the body corporate committee, and not be released as general correspondence.

What else are they hiding? What else have they said against other members of the body corporate?

So I was unable to obtain the name of the author of the request. As stated above; the committee doesn't want their meetings recorded in any way shape or form; and they were quick to hide comments about a member of the body corporate by making them "privileged" under the Act.

In short, committee members like to hide behind anonymity, and they did so with the support of their body corporate managers. There is another word for this: cowardice. My question is, what do they have to hide?

What is a complex manager?

Theory

Complex managers are engaged by the body corporate to look after the day-to-day activities of the complex. They usually reside on site and are responsible for arranging repairs, servicing, and maintaining the cleanliness and running of the complex. They answer to the committee and do whatever the committee wants them to do, within reason. At The Apartments, they also ran the holiday let business for the complex.

Practice

The complex managers at the time I moved in requested permission from the body corporate committee to charge a fee for using the lifts to move furniture and other large items. The fee was to cover their time and effort in hanging protective blankets in the lift, to prevent damage to the lift walls.

Had the committee and body corporate managers done their job competently, they would simply have advised the complex managers that the fee was inappropriate: that protecting the lift during moves was a part of the complex managers' duties under the standard contract and it is never appropriate to charge lot owners for using common property. Instead, a fraudulent fee was foisted on the inhabitants until I challenged it.

3

WHEN THINGS GO WRONG

Although I had heard of corruption within the New South Wales Police Force, at the time I entered the force, it had been dealt with. Much of the problem had been with the tow truck industry. I served in several stations throughout my career, and at none of those stations had I ever been party to, heard of, or witnessed any sort of corruption. In contrast, when I moved into The Apartments, on the very first day I moved in, I became a victim of the corruption at the complex.

CASE STUDY #1:

Fraud in The Apartments

Theory

Cambridge Dictionary defines fraudulent as: "Dishonest and illegal".

Merriam-Webster Dictionary defines fraudulent as: "Characterised by, based on, or done by fraud: Deceitful".

The Queensland *Criminal Code 1899* states:

> **408C Fraud**
>
> 1) A person who dishonestly—
>
>   a) applies to his or her own use or to the use of any person—
>
>   i) property belonging to another; or
>
>   ii) property belonging to the person, or which is in the person's possession, either solely or jointly with another person, subject to a trust, direction or condition or on account of any other person; or
>
>   b) obtains property from any person; or
>
>   c) induces any person to deliver property to any person; or
>
>   d) gains a benefit or advantage, pecuniary or otherwise, for any person; or
>
>   e) causes a detriment, pecuniary or otherwise, to any person; or

f) induces any person to do any act which the person is lawfully entitled to abstain from doing; or

g) induces any person to abstain from doing any act which that person is lawfully entitled to do; or

h) makes off, knowing that payment on the spot is required or expected for any property lawfully supplied or returned or for any service lawfully provided, without having paid and with intent to avoid payment; commits the crime of fraud.

Maximum penalty—5 years imprisonment.

Practice

I was charged a $35 fee when I moved into the complex. The complex managers told me that this was for their work to hang heavy industrial canvas protectors in the elevator, to protect it from damage. They charged this fee to any person moving in or out or having furniture delivered. Like everybody else, I paid it (twice, as I paid for my then partner when she moved into the apartment below mine), not knowing that it was an illegal fee. Now, some people might think I'm making a mountain out of a molehill — it was only $35 — but if a stranger approached you and asked for $35, giving no reason other than, "It's only $35," would you give it to them? I think not. In addition, $35 paid by 74 apartments whenever someone moves in or out adds up to a considerable amount of money over time.

Did they know they were doing something wrong? It's unclear. But this fee had to be paid in cash on the day of moving and no receipts were given.

The following committee members held office during the fraud: Hercules (Chairperson), Artemis (Secretary), Orpheus, Triton, Clotho, Venus, and Athena.

I only found out that the fee was illegal because another resident queried it. To check, all I did was make a single phone call to the BCCM information service, and they informed me that complex managers cannot charge for using common property. There are seven body corporate committee members and a body corporate manager; it appears that none of them bothered to check whether the fee was appropriate. The intention to commit fraud, in my view, lies in the fact that all the responsible parties failed to ascertain the legality of the fee being charged.

From the time I first applied to have the fees I'd paid reimbursed to the time of the conciliation about the matter was approximately four months. During that time, not one other person made that same fact-finding phone call.

CONCILIATION #1:

The rip-off

Theory

When a lot owner has an issue, for example, when their apartment needs repairs, the lot owner applies to the committee to have the matter tabled and dealt with. The committee then decides whether to approve or deny that request.

If the lot owner disagrees with the decision by the committee, the matter then can go to the Office of the Commissioner for Body Corporate and Community Management in the capital city, in my case, Brisbane. First though, the parties have to follow a self-resolution process, that is, the lot owner and the committee are supposed to resolve the matter by themselves.

If they can't resolve it, the lot owner may apply to have the matter heard at the Office of the Commissioner. Both the lot owner and selected member/s of the committee attend the offices to deal with the matter in consultation with a Conciliator. Once a resolution to the matter is agreed upon, both parties leave.

Unfortunately, the conciliation is **not** a binding agreement. If one of the parties does not do whatever was agreed upon, the other party can request an adjudication. This, of course, is another application with more costs involved. Even then, an adjudication order does not have to be complied with.

If still unresolved, the matter goes to the Queensland Civil and Administrative Tribunal. The whole process is both lengthy and costly.

Practice

To establish to the body corporate committee's satisfaction that the complex managers had been charging an illegal fee, I had to engage this tortuous dispute resolution process, as it is specified in the BCCM Act.

First, as a resident, I put an application to the committee in writing to establish the facts. In this case, I applied for the body corporate committee to acknowledge that the $35 fee charged by the complex managers for protecting the elevator during moves should never have been charged. I had actually met privately with the then chairperson to discuss the matter. This was the self-resolution process.

As this initial application was rejected, the next step was a more formal request, tabled at the next committee meeting. As this request was also rejected, I had to complete a Form 15, Conciliation Application, and lodge it with the Office of the Commissioner in Brisbane, at a cost of approximately $70. BCCM assigned it to a Conciliator, who must attempt to resolve the matter with the disputing parties. The whole process takes a minimum of three months. I applied for conciliation, and due to the simplicity of this matter, the Conciliator was able to handle it over the phone.

After this long and complicated process, there were still further hoops to jump through. Anyone who wanted to be reimbursed had to approach the complex managers and wait. Although the money was demanded at the time of moving in and in cash only, it took several weeks to be reimbursed by cheque. The complex managers did not automatically or voluntarily reimburse the residents who had paid the illegal fee: each resident had to apply for their refund.

As for me, I'd spent $70 — and a lot of time and energy — to regain $70 and do what I thought was right.

CASE STUDY #2:
Budget deficit

Theory

The body corporate levies its members to fund the common expenses: building and public liability insurance; cleaning and maintenance of the common areas; running the body corporate itself; etc. So they are entrusted with everyone's money, sometimes in quite large amounts.

When the budget went into deficit, it was due to over-expenditure on legal fees. The BCCM Act states the committee's spending limit is $200 per issue per lot. For The Apartments this means a total of $14,800. However, the original owner had raised the limit to $500 per lot, meaning the committee can spend up to $37,000 without special approval of the body corporate. The increase had never been reduced. And the committee were willing to spend up to and over that limit on legal fees!

As the committee had put the budget into deficit, I submitted a motion to reduce the limit again in accordance with the Act. The body corporate approved this, and the limit was reduced. But the very next year, the committee submitted their own motion to have it increased again, which was approved by the body corporate.

On yet another occasion, the committee wanted to raise a further $75,000 for more legal fees in a special levy, due to a dispute with the owner of the café at the front of the building over an exhaust fan.

I'm glad I don't trust my money with them anymore.

Practice

This was the second conciliation I requested. It dealt with the fact that the committee had allowed the budget to go into deficit. Again, there were multiple reasons I felt I had to act: first, some of the money being squandered was mine; second, the deficit constituted another offence under the BCCM Act; and third, the committee was caught transferring money between accounts to make the budget appear to be out of deficit.

I would not trust my money with that type of dishonest committee. It certainly made me wonder why the budget went into deficit in the first place!

CASE STUDY #3:

The case of the weeping walls

Theory

If there is something to be repaired on common property, it is the responsibility of the body corporate to arrange to have it fixed. So the committee, working with the complex managers, are supposed to arrange to have whatever it is repaired at the cost of the body corporate. For example, the water that was leaking from foundations into my exclusive use car space, or the water damage to my kitchen from a leak in the balcony above mine, were both items for which the body corporate is responsible; however, a lot owner must apply to the committee to have the particular item/s repaired.

Practice

The third conciliation dealt with water leaking into my exclusive use car space. The carpark was designed with wet walls, that is, walls designed to seep, delivering any excess water into a trench below the wet wall and then diverting it to a drain. But the trench and drainage was not able to cope with the amount of water seeping through the walls in this area. At times I had to stand in water to get in or out of my vehicle, or access the boot. This had been an ongoing matter since I moved into the apartment, however nothing was done to fix it, though it had been on the agenda for years: I kept submitting requests for the drainage to be corrected.

About five years later, when still nothing had been done, I purchased four rubber mats on which to park my vehicle, keeping the tyres and wheels out of the water. I thought this was a fair effort to find a friendly solution to at least part of the problem. The total cost of the rubber mats was $34.50. Yet my request for reimbursement was denied, as noted in the May Year 6 minutes (correspondence).

There were three problems with this, from my perspective.

First, how petty! It was a trifling sum — slightly less than the fraudulent fee the committee, body corporate managers and complex managers had expected residents to overlook.

Second, I obtained notes that my request was rejected on the basis that I hadn't applied to be reimbursed for the mats **prior** to purchasing them. However, there were at least two occasions on which lot owners had been reimbursed for expenses despite not have applied in advance. Two owners had been reimbursed $231 and $187 respectively for money they had spent on water ingress repairs for common property windows that affected them. Correspondence in the Year 1 May minutes shows that the full committee approved their requests. Of course, one owner was a committee member at the time, and it might have been just a little too obvious to approve one request, but not the other.

On another occasion, the complex managers had also been approved to be reimbursed the sum of $1,793, for legal expenses, after the event. So a precedent was well and truly established.

Third and last, in the minutes of the committee meeting that rejected my application for reimbursement, I noticed that only the executive members of the committee voted on the matter. But partial voting of the committee is illegal. Again, the committee had breached the BCCM Act and ECS had allowed it to occur against their own code of conduct. It appears, from the minutes, that committee member Hera was present, but the executive members were the only people who voted. This is particularly confusing, as Hera had voted on the reimbursements for two apartments. Why did she neither say nor do anything? Why did she not even vote? The members who did vote were Apollo (Chairperson), Venus (Secretary) and Freya (Treasurer).

Many months later, as part of the conciliation in August Year 6, the committee finally agreed to fix the water ingress problem into the car park. They agreed that the amount of $20,000 would be put aside to complete the job. But by the time I sold my apartment in February Year 8, the problem still had not been fixed. The committee had not even complied with their own agreement.

CASE STUDY #4:

The infamous toilet paper saga

It was not beneath the committee, with the assistance of ECS who forwarded me the correspondence, to infer that I was a thief. I have absolutely no idea why they undertook this endeavour. Whether it was an attempt to intimidate me, prove that they have the authority, or a warning, I do not know. However, they did it, and here we are.

I am also puzzled to imagine what incentive the committee could have given the body corporate managers who tried to ruin my Christmas. My body corporate fees increased by over 31% in the space of two years, which is yet another breach of the legislation, as body corporate levies are not supposed to increase or decrease by more than 10% annually. And the committee had done illegal things with body corporate funds previously, with no consequences …

Theory

Common property is for the enjoyment for all building users: owner–occupiers, renters, friends, guests, and holiday makers alike. This includes the toilets in the common area. Body corporate funds are used to maintain the common property and these funds are all supplied by lot owners through both regular and special body corporate levies.

As a full financial member of The Apartments' body corporate, I was entitled to use the common areas, including the consumables supplied for common use. Since I lived on the seventh floor, it would have cost more to use the elevator to go up to my apartment than to use the common toilets, or toilet paper from them.

Practice

I received correspondence via ECS dated 22 December Year 2 (a mere 3 days before Christmas). The committee had instructed them to forward me correspondence in relation to security images dated 16 December Year 2. In those images you can see I am exiting the common area toilets on the mezzanine level, holding approximately five sheets of a roll of toilet paper. You're shocked, aren't you?

This means that, in the busy festive season, in the 6 days from 16 December when the images were taken, to 22 December when the correspondence was dated, the committee took the following actions:

1) Received the downloaded images from the security system from the then complex managers.

2) Organised and held a "voting outside committee meeting", discussed and voted on the matter.

3) Wrote an accusatory letter to me.

4) Forwarded the letter and the security images via ECS to me.

The committee that couldn't fix a simple drainage prob-lem in seven years achieved this whole process in six days, including a weekend; the DC Comics hero, The Flash, doesn't go that quick!

The committee had passed the following resolution:

> The committee resolves that, having exam-ined several security images which identify a unit owner entering the community toilets and leaving 23 seconds later carrying what appears to be a quantity of toilet paper, the unit owner be contacted and requested to comment on the security images.

Let me repeat, I was holding five squares of a single roll of toilet paper. I calculated the cost of that paper to be approximately 8 cents. Yet it would have cost the body corporate approximately $500 for this committee meet-ing to take place and to organise the paperwork. That is not very financially responsible.

As a lot owner, I was a financial member of The Apartments' body corporate, and entitled to use the com-mon areas, including any consumables supplied.

And what did I use this toilet paper for? It was to wipe up an oil drop from in front of my car after I did a fluid check. Although there is a light in my parking area, it was blocked by the open bonnet of my car, so I had to walk onto the common property, oil stick in hand, to check the level showing on my dipstick. In short, I was cleaning up an oil spot on common property.

What part of the Act, or BCCM's code of conduct, did my behaviour breach? The committee was breaching clauses 2(1) and 3, and ECS clauses 4 and 6, of their respective codes of conduct.

The following committee members were responsible for this incident: Hercules (Chairperson), Venus (Secretary), Athena (Treasurer), Orpheus, Triton, Clotho, and Hermes.

CASE STUDY #5:

Call your lawyers

As you might imagine, I felt I needed to respond to this despicable incident. After considerable thought, I proposed a motion to issue the body corporate's Secretary with a breach notice.

The then Chairperson, Zeus, ruled that the motion was out of order. He based this on section 79 (1)(a) of the Accommodation Module. Section 79 lets a Chairperson rule a motion out of order based on a conflict with other parts of the legislation or by-laws, that it has already been voted on, or similar procedural reasons. The reason minuted was that it was unenforceable. But in the minutes of the meeting it does not specify why it would be unenforceable.

The committee referred my motion to their lawyers — paying for their advice with body corporate levies. As you've read, when a member of the body corporate applies for a conciliation, they must first deal with the committee and the body corporate managers. In this case, it soon became obvious I would have to deal with a bunch of lawyers as well. The advice from Loki Lawyers (not their real name) stated:

> It [the motion] fails to sufficiently identify who any notice is to be issued to. Granted the motion requires a notice to be issued to the "Secretary" but the secretary at the conclusion of the meeting may not be the secre-

> tary Mr Andrew in fact wishes a notice to be served on. Indeed, the situation could arise where Mr Andrew is elected secretary for the Scheme. In which case, where the motion is favourably resolved the Body Corporate would be required to issue a notice to Mr Andrew.
>
> It fails to sufficiently identify the alleged breaches of the Code of Conduct, such that it is uncertain without investigation whether the Code of Conduct indeed had been breached.

The lawyers were probably not given complete information in their brief, because the motion, with the addition of its supporting material, quite effectively establishes and outlines the breaches of the code of conduct committed by the Secretary, Venus. It includes everything from photographic evidence of the infamous toilet paper saga to the falsifying of records: it is all in the motion.

As a result of the emails that are in my possession, I emailed Loki Lawyers, asking why they gave advice to ECS on how to have my motion ruled out of order, and why they used my name as an example. Extracts from my enquiry are below.

> … I am in the process of writing a book about my experiences at [The Apartments], focusing on the committee.

... I submitted a motion to be tabled at the Annual General Meeting in that the Secretary was to be issued a breach notice for breaching the Code of Conduct. [Loki Lawyers'] response was that the motion was not clear as to who the breach notice was to be issued to although it does mention the Secretary. Therefore the motion must be ruled out of order as it was unenforceable. No other reason was given. I now find it interesting that that particular part of the legislation is going to be amended so that the Chairperson must provide a reason.

I am wondering if [Loki Lawyers] in fact received the full information ... As a retired police officer from NSW, it was my job to submit briefs of evidence to several courts of law including lower courts, district and coroners' courts. I have perused the motion and all its supporting material, and I cannot find any deficiency in the motion and am at a loss at to why that advice was given. Although I do not have at hand the author of that advice, [Mr Fenrir], is mentioned in similar correspondence.

In the interest of fairness, this is giving [Loki Lawyers] the opportunity to provide a response as to why that advice was given. A response, if any, may or may not be quoted in my book.

Clearly they were not impressed, as I received the following reply from the head honcho:

> Mr Andrew
>
> We refer to your email below, which has been passed on to me to respond to as the managing director of the firm.
>
> … you ought to be aware that advice given by a solicitor to its client is the subject of legal professional privilege. That privilege:
>
> 1) Subsists in a client, not the solicitor; and
>
> 2) Prevents the solicitor from disseminating the advice to any person but the client, without the client's specific consent or the client otherwise waiving the privilege.
>
> Do you have the Body Corporate's consent for us to provide that advice to you or to otherwise waive the privilege? Alternately, do you have clear proof that the Body Corporate has already waived privilege in the advice?
>
> If you do not, then we are simply unable to provide any information to you to the extent it relates to the advice given.
>
> Although you say you are of the view there is no deficiency in the relevant Motion, we

respectfully suggest you seek independent legal advice on the matter.

Finally, as you have indicated you intend to publish a book in respect of the body corporate matters (including the ruling of the relevant motion out of order) and you have indicated that you are aware this firm has provided advice to the body corporate, our firm hereby reserves its rights and [Mr Fenrir] reserves his rights, respectively, in respect of any statements you make about our firm and/or [Mr Fenrir].

We strongly recommend you seek independent legal advice in respect of the matter.

Regards

[Name withheld], Legal Practitioner Director

Before the annual general meeting (AGM), the Secretary had replied to the motion that I had submitted. It clearly states this in the explanatory schedules, which were part of the annual general meeting paperwork. So Venus knew all along that my motion was submitted as a result of her behaviour. And since this is the case, how could the lawyers state that the motion did not sufficiently identify to whom it was directed? So the Chairperson ruled the motion out of order based on not sufficiently identifying who the Secretary was, even though he must have known, as it was in the paperwork before the AGM.

The reference to me possibly becoming the Secretary one day also baffled me. I had at that time never been on the committee, and therefore was not subject to the code of conduct for committee members, so it would have been impossible for me to be issued a breach notice. In fact, the Secretary that the breach notice was directed at, Venus, had been the **only** Secretary for several years. So taking that into consideration, and the fact that the Secretary replied to the motion before the AGM, how did Zeus get away with ruling the motion out of order. **Seriously?**

Maybe Loki Lawyers did not get the full story from either ECS or the committee when this particular incident was referred to them. However, a bit of investigation on their part, instead of accusing me of lack of investigation, would have been a prudent direction to take.

The legislation changed in early 2021. There have been too many incidents of this type. Now that the amendments have been made, when a chairperson rules a motion out of order they have to supply a reason why it is being ruled out of order.

4

CONCLUSION — APOLOGY?

In the end, I sold my unit and moved out. I live in a nice peaceful house now. The neighbours are fine, and we all let each other be.

In this book, I have outlined the deceitful, illegal, and nasty things that The Apartments's body corporate committee, with the assistance of ECS, did over the years I lived there. It included everything from allowing the complex managers to rip off the residents by charging an illegal fee, to falsifying records, to the spurious and false accusations of the toilet paper saga. And I haven't even included most of the plainly ridiculous things they did or tried to do, such as putting forward a motion that every resident and guest had to be off their balcony by 10pm every night. I mean, you couldn't make this stuff up!

And yet, during Year 7, I was asked to apologise to the committee! How does that work? Honestly, I laughed so hard I nearly wet myself!

I strongly believe that a royal commission into the body corporate and community management industry would not be out of place.

About the author

Michael Andrew was raised with love and discipline in a military family in Sydney's western suburbs. He entered the NSW Police Force straight after high school, and enjoyed the adrenaline rush of running down the road and crash-tackling an armed offender who'd just robbed a bank. His greatest honour was the rescue of a rock fisherman at North Palm Beach, for which he was awarded a certificate of bravery from the NSW Royal Humane Society. After 21 years' service, Michael was medically discharged from the police force.

Michael's greatest achievement, however, is raising his daughter — now an adult. He does not like bullies, or anyone who takes advantage of others, preferring animals and kids.

www.ingramcontent.com/pod-product-compliance
Lightning Source LLC
Chambersburg PA
CBHW051008050726
47592CB00007B/2758